WHY BABIES DO THAT

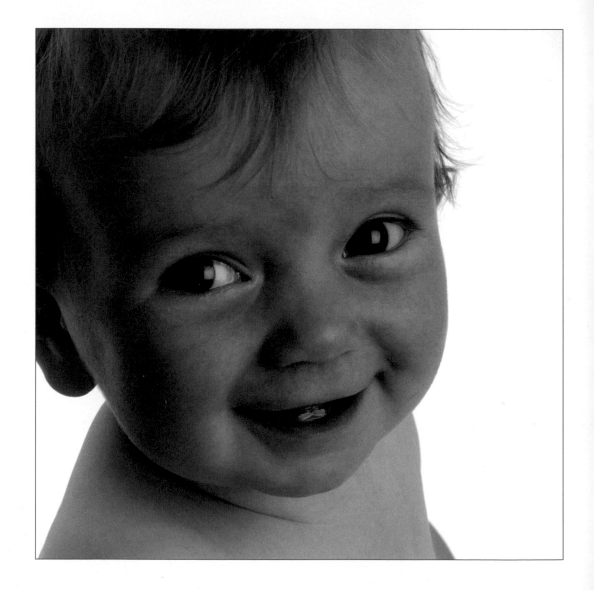

WHY BABIES DO THAT

BAFFLING BABY BEHAVIOR EXPLAINED

JENNIFER MARGULIS

WILLOW CREEK PRESS

Text © 2005 Jennifer Margulis

All photographs © 2005 Paul Franz except the following:
     page 11 © Tom & Dee Ann McCarthy/Corbis; page 16 © Larry Williams
     & Associates/zefa/Corbis; page 26 © Norvia Behling; page 30 © RF/Corbis;
     page 36 © Whiskey Tango/Corbis; page 38 © Jim Craigmyle/Corbis;
     page 68 © RF; page 90 © Norvia Behling; page 94 © Norvia Behling;
     page 96 © RF

Published by Willow Creek Press
P.O. Box 147, Minocqua, Wisconsin 54548

Editor/Design: Andrea K. Donner

Library of Congress Cataloging-in-Publication Data
Margulis, Jennifer.
   Why babies do that : a book of baffling baby behaviors explained / text by
Jennifer Margulis.
          p. cm.
   ISBN 1-59543-243-4 (hardcover : alk. paper)
   1. Child psychology. 2. Infants. I. Title.
   HQ772.M248 2005
   305.231--dc22
                                                        2005016326

Printed in Canada

For James, the best baby tamer and most

curious quirky father I know;

and for Etani Autumn, the gentlest, most patient

and most affable baby in the world.

—J.M.

For my daughters, Isabella and Jocelyn,

who helped inspire me while working

on the photographs for this book.

—P.F.

Table of Contents

Preface

As soft, warm, and cuddly as they are, babies are strange creatures. Many newborns emerge into the world with cone-shaped heads, half-closed eyes, and wrinkled, peeling skin. Some even have acne. As they grow, they continue to make funny noises, they find specs of dust in the air so fascinating they will cross their eyes to follow them, they enjoy sucking on their own toes, and they cough, splutter, spit up, and drool... usually all over us.

Yet these tiny, quirky creatures who generate so many loads of laundry and so completely disrupt our sleep somehow manage to thoroughly endear themselves to us. Not only do we fall deeply in love with them, we find ourselves checking on them twenty-seven times an hour when they are sleeping, emptying our wallets to buy them the latest gizmos and gadgets, talking to them in a high-pitched, sing-song voice that would make our former (skinnier,

hipper) selves cringe, and generally behaving in a baffling manner, all for the sake of a baby.

As babies grow and mature, we adults in their lives change too. We realize that the only constant in a baby's babyhood is change. We learn that a baby behavior we can find adorable one minute can exasperate us the next (however sweet it is to watch a baby pick up his first raisin and however funny it is the first time he flings that raisin half way across the kitchen, after the 252nd time you reach for the broom, it doesn't hold quite as much charm). We also discover that babies are bewildering; they do many quirky things that seem inexplicable to both the novice parent and the seasoned grandparent (and to everyone else in between, especially the lady behind you in the grocery store on whose shirt your baby just spat up).

That's where *Why Babies Do That* comes in. Without attempting to be exhaustive (one look at the parenting section will show you that it takes a bookstore to raise a child), we have tried to elucidate many of the key behaviors that you may encounter in your dealings with babies. The babies discussed in this book are between zero and one year of age (if you're dying to know about older babies, stay tuned for the next book on toddlers). The behaviors explained in this book range from the truly bizarre (why do babies play with their own poop?) to the truly lovable (why do babies love to be cuddled?) and everything in between.

As you read the text and enjoy the pictures, it is important to keep in mind that babies, like adults, are highly individual, and that not all babies will behave in the ways mentioned here. When we indicate the age that a baby does something, that is an average only. Do not worry if your baby does things on his own timeline. One friend's baby did virtually nothing for the first full year he was born. He smiled. He cooed. He looked around. That was about all.

Reading baby books made his mother worry that something was terribly wrong with her son. He has since grown up to be a strapping, smart, and successful young man. Of course, if your baby is exhibiting a really bizarre behavior, or if you're worried, you should not hesitate to seek help from a health care professional or an experienced friend. The doctor my husband called at 2:00 in the morning when my newborn pooped her fourth seedy, mustardy poop in ten minutes—the one who told us diarrhea is extremely rare in breast fed babies— reassured us that we had done well to check in with her.

Once they master one skill, babies often discard it and move onto another. In photographs and prose, *Why Babies Do That* captures some of a baby's finest, albeit fleeting, moments. As much as this book is meant to inform you about baby behaviors, it is also meant to inspire you… to play peek-a-boo with, cuddle, bounce, and enjoy all of the babies in your life.

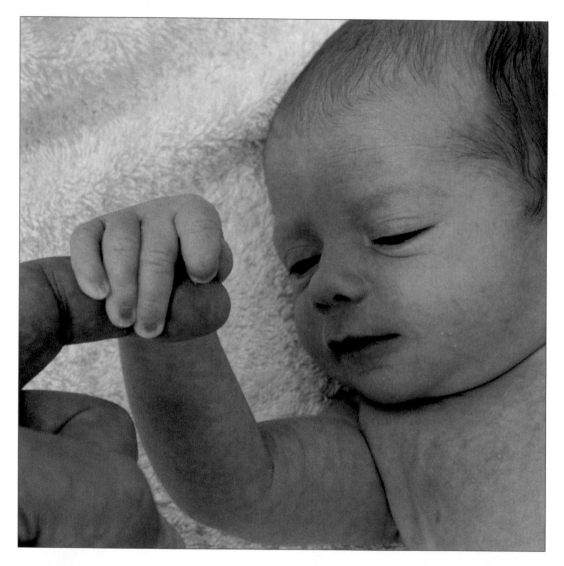

Why Babies Do That

Why Do Babies Grasp Onto Things So Tightly?

One minutes-old baby I knew grabbed her mother's shirt so tightly that two nurses could not pry her away to weigh and measure her. They decided to try again later. The grasping reflex is one of many reflexes babies are born with. If you put your finger in the palm of a newborn's hand, she will usually clamp her tiny fingers onto yours. A newborn's grip is so strong that she can actually support her own weight. Some scientists have hypothesized that human babies have inherited this reflex from primates, and the instinct to cling tightly to safety has obvious survival benefits. A recent study of full-term newborns also showed that babies' heartbeats decelerate when they grasp onto their mothers, suggesting that the newborns get a sense of security from grasping tightly to their mothers, which actually calms them down.

As the baby grows, she replaces the involuntary grasping reflex with a keen interest in trying to control her movements and grab onto things. At about three months of age a baby will be able to bat objects that dangle in front of her, and some time after that she will be able to grab them and hold them tightly. Five-month-old babies will delight in lying on their backs and swatting at their own elusive feet, clutching them tightly. The movement of grasping, at this age, is now under the control of the cerebral cortex, the part of our brains that controls our willed behavior.

Once babies master the skill of grasping and are able to negotiate such fascinating activities as spoon-holding and sippy-cup-against-the-high-chair whacking, beware: they move on to dropping, throwing, and letting go of everything in sight. Except, that is, when a coveted toy is threatened to be taken by an older sibling or a baby friend, in which case they rediscover their iron grip. Whoever said taking candy from a baby is easy has never tried.

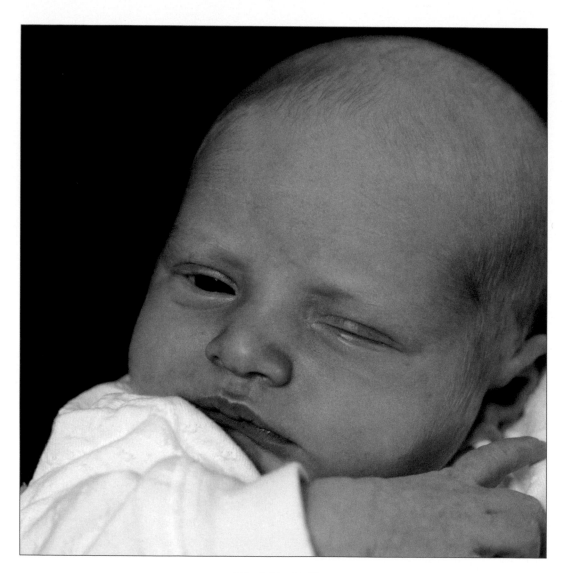

Why Babies Do That

Why Do Some Newborns Open Only One Eye at a Time, Cross Their Eyes, or Roll Their Eyes Back?

Eyesight is the least developed of all the newborn senses. Until they are about three months old, infants see best in their peripheral vision. A newborn can only see clearly about eight to twelve inches in front of him (the exact distance to bring his mother or father into focus).

Combine poor vision with the tiring experience of birth and you've got the answer to why an infant's eyes act so strangely. A newborn has gone through quite an ordeal—being squeezed through the birth canal and pushed out into the world. He then must acquire sustenance out of a breast that is twice the size of his head. It's exhausting! And those eyelids are heavy. So if you're that tired, why bother opening two myopic eyes when you can just open one (and then close it again and go back to sleep)?

Once they do manage to open both eyes for more than a few seconds, it's very common for an infant's eyes to wander independently or cross as she tries to look at something. While disturbing for us caregivers, this is perfectly normal. For the first six months, an infant's brain is working hard to teach the eyes how to work together to see things. Once she learns to do this, her eyes will stop crossing. Additionally, babies have large epicanthal folds (the skin of the upper eyelid that partially covers the inner corner of the eye) and flat noses to allow for easier breastfeeding. These folds cover the inner corners of a baby's eyes and sometimes give the impression that the eyes are crossing even though they are not.

When a newborn is in a light sleep her eyelids might flutter, allowing us the uncanny experience of seeing her eyes moving underneath the lids. A sleepy baby's eyelids may droop and her eyes roll back in her head, but don't rush to the nearest hospital. It may be weird to watch but it's all perfectly normal.

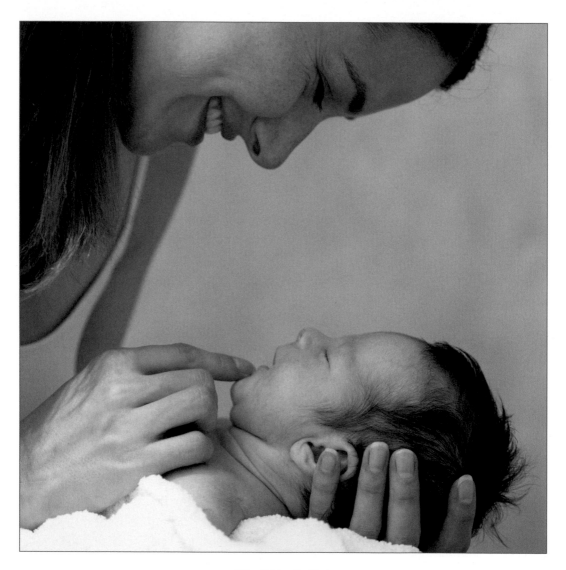

Why Babies Do That

Why Do Newborn Babies Turn Their Heads Toward the Sound of Their Mom or Dad's Voice?

I remember taking my two-day-old to the doctor for a routine check-up, disrobing her, and laying her on the examining table. She fussed and held my finger in her strong grip. As I started talking to her, she quieted right down, turning her head toward the sound of my voice.

Studies have shown that newborns prefer the sound of human voices to any other noise. The familiar voice of a parent is calming to a newborn baby. In the first few weeks of development in utero, an embryo's external ear begins forming, and by the sixth month a fetus can hear, albeit not perfectly. In addition to your heartbeat and the internal sounds in the womb, a baby in utero also hears the sound of your voice, and the sound of other people's voices around you, though not as well. Since humans do not have large and easily moveable external ears to help locate the direction from which a sound is coming (like dogs do, for example), we localize the source of a sound by the slight differences in the arrival time of the sound in each ear. Babies, like adults, turn their heads toward the source of a sound in order to ascertain from where it is emanating. A newborn who turns his head toward you when you speak is both recognizing your voice and locating your whereabouts.

A newborn will also turn his face in your direction with his mouth open and root, or search for food, if you stroke the side of his cheek gently. This movement is motivated by your touch, not your voice. It is called the *rooting reflex* and it is a way to insure that newborns do not starve. If you are touching a baby's cheek and talking to him at the same time, he may be responding to one stimulus or the other.

Why Babies Do That

Why Do Babies Form Attachments to Blankies or Special Stuffies?

A dog-eared blankie, a hand-me-down Big Bird—many babies find comfort and love from one special inanimate object. She may always want this comfort object with her or may only look for her special blankie or stuffie at naptime, bedtime, or when she hurts herself. My little sister's stuffed doggie was so dear to her that she learned to say its name, "Didi," before she learned any other word.

You know how nice it feels at the end of a long day to climb between your favorite flannel sheets, pull up the comforter, and bury your head in the pillow? The sense of peace and well-being that comes from a familiar ritual in familiar surroundings is how a baby feels when she hugs her special stuffie. Everything about the comfort item is familiar—its musty smell, its satin trim that is just right to rub between two fingers, its color and feel. Having a security blanket, like thumb sucking, is a way for a baby to find confidence and comfort by herself. Although some parents may worry that these items foster dependent behavior, the opposite is probably closer to the truth; a baby who has a special attachment to a special stuffie or blankie is finding a way to make the world outside of her parents' protection a less overwhelming place. Comfort objects are especially common among young babies who spend long hours in daycare. Having something familiar and unchanging to snuggle against helps them while they are away from home.

No matter how dirty or ragged a baby's comfort object might seem to you, resist the temptation to wash it or replace it with a new one. A baby loves its unique smell and tatteredness. The comfort object also absorbs the baby's own scent, making it familiar territory. That's part of what makes it so special.

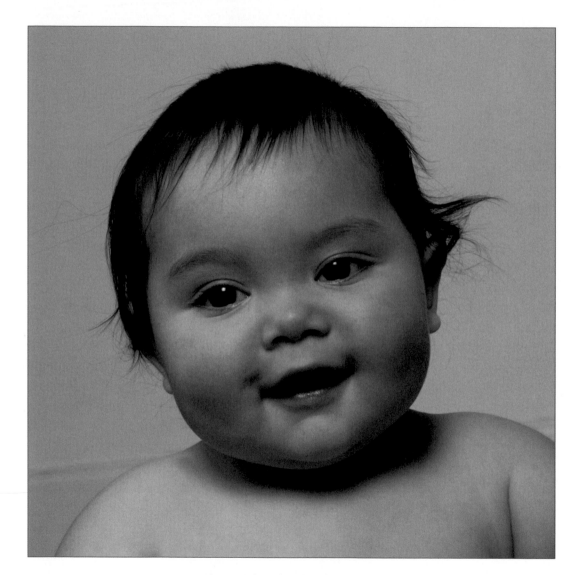

Why Babies Do That

Why Do Some Babies Have Lots of Hair on Their Heads and Others None at All?

Unlike other primates who sport thick fur coats, we humans only have a light covering of hair over our bodies. However, by the sixth month the fetus in utero is actually covered all over with short unpigmented hairs (called *lanugo*). Premature babies are sometimes born with lanugo, though it will fall out in a matter of weeks after birth.

What does all this have to do with head hair? By the sixth month in utero a baby's hair follicles and the glands in the follicles that secrete an oily substance to keep the hair and skin soft are fully formed. There are about 100,000 hair follicles on the scalp but as a person ages many of these follicles stop growing hair. Much of what else that is known about human baby hair is specu-lation. Some babies are still completely bald when they hit their first birthdays. Others have long thick hair (and tangles to comb). This is probably because some babies have hair that grows much more slowly than others. It is thought that hormones and heredity influence these hair growth patterns.

Interestingly, scientists think that it is the shape of the hair follicle that dictates if a baby's hair will be straight or curly (round follicles grow straight hair; oval or crescent-shaped follicles grow frizzy hair). If you have a com-pletely bald baby in your life, you may be reassured to know that the pattern of baby hair growth does not determine how thick or long an older child's hair will be.

Why Babies Do That

Why Do Most Babies Lose the Hair They Are Born With?

Some babies are born with a full head of downy, black hair. Others are born completely bald (though if you look closely you can see that they actually have some very fine hair on their pates). Don't be fooled by the texture and the color of your new baby's hair. Though this does not happen with all babies, most newborns will lose all the hair they are born with in the first three or four months of life. At the same time, most new mothers find big clumps of hair in the shower drain and on their brushes. Why such a hirsute exodus?

In order to understand the prevailing theory behind infant hair loss, we need to have a crash course in how hair grows. Just like a baby's maturing body, hair will grow for several months and then take a break from growing. During this resting phase, known by specialists as the *telogen phase*, the bulb at the end of the hair root gets smaller and the hair becomes loose. For an adult, ten to fifteen percent of hair can be in the telogen phase, while the rest of the hair is still growing. For a newborn, however, all of the hair is thought to go into the telogen phase at once, resulting in complete hair loss. While the reasons for this are not entirely understood, researchers speculate that it has to do with the sharp decline in exposure to sex hormones after birth. That decline is also thought to be the reason a pregnant woman sheds her once beautiful hair after giving birth.

Babies can also become bald for other reasons. If a baby always sleeps in one position, the rubbing of his head on the mattress will result in localized baldness. Less commonly, ringworm—a fungal infection—on the scalp can result in hair loss.

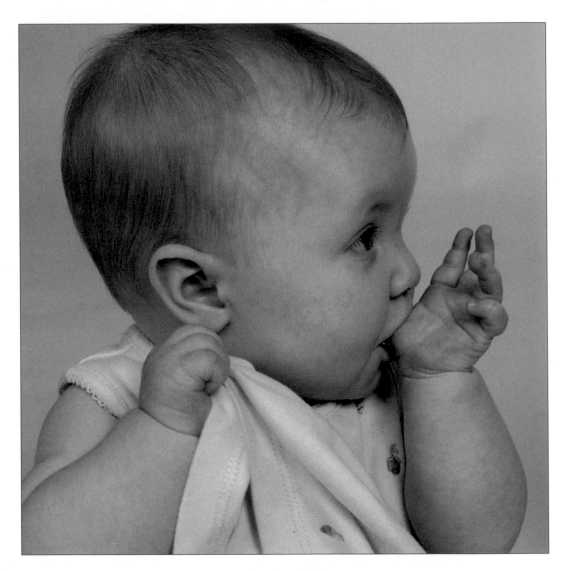

Why Babies Do That

Why Do Babies Suck Their Thumbs?

Most babies have a very strong need for what is called *non-nutritive sucking*, that is, sucking that does not provide them with food. They suck on their thumbs, on their fingers, on their fists, on pacifiers, on your pinky finger held upside down in their mouths (cut your fingernails first), on you (ever noticed a big purplish red welt on your arm after you've been carrying a baby over your shoulder for a while and not been sure where it came from? Look no further). Ultrasound advancements have also shown that some babies even begin sucking their thumbs or fingers by the fifth month in the womb.

There are several reasons why a baby sucks her thumb. A baby's mouth is her most sensitive organ at birth, as well as the one over which she has the most control. The need to suck is one of our most basic survival instincts and a baby who has a strong sucking reflex will have less trouble latching on to a nipple to nurse than a baby who has a weaker sucking reflex. Thumb sucking is also a deeply calming activity for a baby, helping him to relax and feel secure. A hungry baby may suck lustily on his thumb if no food is forthcoming as a way to stave off hunger.

As a baby gets older, thumb sucking becomes an interesting activity. Babies learn about the world by putting things in their mouths, and tasting and experiencing their environment. An older baby may be fascinated by his hands and fingers—putting them in his mouth is another way to explore them.

Should you worry about a baby sucking his thumb? Absolutely not. Think of it as a pacifier that cannot get lost and be happy that your baby has discovered a self-soothing technique on her own.

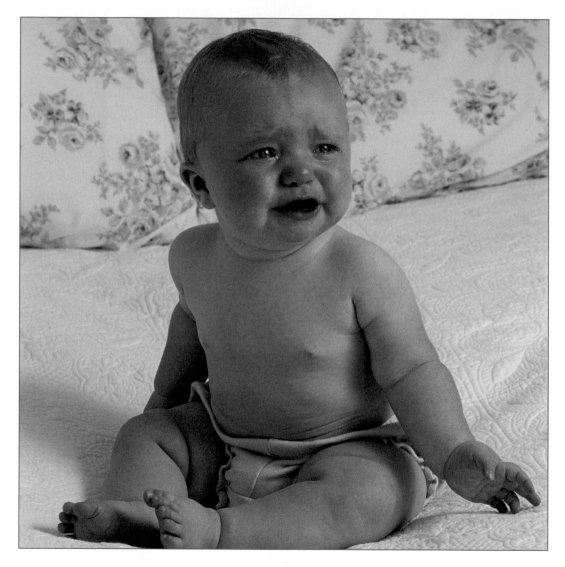

Why Babies Do That

Why Do Babies Cry?

If I could give one definitive answer to this question it would be like revealing the whereabouts of the Fountain of Youth. We all know that babies cry because they can't talk and they need to communicate to us that something is wrong—they are hungry, tired, wet, uncomfortable, in pain, or wanting to be held. Even though some parents, especially mothers, discover early on that their baby's cry changes depending on what the little one needs, one of the hardest things about becoming a parent is trying to figure out why your baby is crying, and what to do about it.

It is quite common for newborns to be inconsolable. Some newborns seem to cry all the time except when they are nursing or sleeping. While healthcare professionals theorize that these babies have some kind of digestive disorder (and label them "colicky"), there is no scientific evidence that proves a disorder called colic exists. Recently, a new theory about fussy babies surmises that because babies' heads need to be small enough to fit through the birth canal, their brain development takes place at astonishing rates during the first three months of life outside of the womb. Some researchers believe that overstimulation outside of the womb is what causes babies to cry continuously for the first three months, after which the crying usually tapers off. A "new" method of soothing a crying baby is to simulate womb-like conditions—wrapping the baby tightly, jiggling her on your knees, making the *swoosh swoosh* sounds from the womb, etc. (sounds like grandma's method, doesn't it?).

Other methods to soothe a baby include going for a walk, dancing with the baby in your arms to soothing music, soaking in the tub together, or handing the baby off to a less tired pair of loving arms.

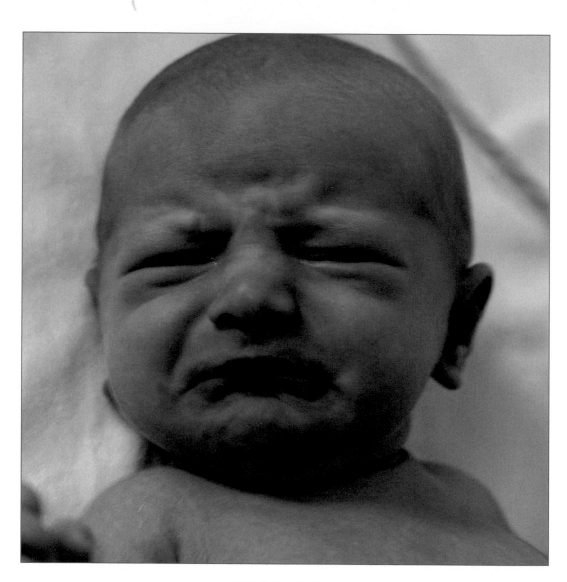

Why Babies Do That

Why Do Babies Cry Without Tears?

There are two reasons a baby cries without tears: 1) he's a newborn; 2) he's upset enough to cry out but not upset enough to have tears in his eyes.

Newborns are born with both *basal tearing*—their eyes produce just enough tears to keep the eyes moist and healthy—and *reflex tearing*—their eyes respond to an irritant, like an eyelash, by tearing up. However, babies are not born with *psychic tearing*—tearing that indicates emotional distress.

Although newborns are physiologically able to produce tears, they almost always cry without tears. No one knows exactly why this is, though some propose it is because newborns have blocked or immature tear ducts. Although blocked tear ducts are extremely common in babies (and 90 percent clear up on their own by age one), the symptom of this problem is usually not a lack of tears but an excess of tearing, even when a baby is not upset. If a newborn's tears are flowing over his eyelid instead of down the sides of his face, he probably has blocked ducts.

Between two and four months of age, a baby will start crying with tears in his eyes when he is really upset. A trigger—hunger, loneliness—will cause the baby's nervous system to stimulate the cranial nerve in the brain that will in turn send a message to the tear glands. You may notice, however, that even though your baby can and does cry with tears, often he cries without any tears. In this case, your baby is communicating some kind of distress that is not acute enough to make tears fall. He has woken up from a nap and is calling out for you to come get him; he has lost a toy under the couch and needs your help to retrieve it; he wants you to pick him up. Your baby is not sobbing in pain, fear, or hunger, but instead using his cry to talk to you about something that's wrong, though it's not a dire problem.

Why Babies Do That

Why Do Some Babies Shriek in Terror When a Stranger Tries to Pick Them Up?

A baby usually only shrieks when grandpa (who is supposed to be helping you with a down payment on a house) or your boss (who is considering you for a promotion) tries to pick up the baby! (Just kidding.) *Stranger anxiety*, as this reaction is called, can actually set in at any age, though it usually hits full force when a baby starts crawling. Even a baby as young as two or three months may cry when a stranger picks him up—perhaps because he can sense that the stranger is nervous about holding him or because the stranger has an unfamiliar smell. When a baby of any age cries in someone else's arms, it is usually because he has formed a strong, healthy attachment to his primary caregivers. He can distinguish them from other people and he associates his well-being with them, whereas he does not know what kind of treatment to expect from a stranger. After all, how would you feel if someone you had never seen before picked you up and hugged you?

Once a baby can crawl or walk on his own, he may become particularly clingy and fussy, and may show a more marked fear of strangers. While some babies only frown, pout, or bury their heads when strangers enter the room or try to hold them, other babies at this age will shriek terribly, with tears running down their cheeks, as if in horrible pain. The severity of the baby's reaction depends on his temperament in general and his mood at that particular moment, but researchers believe that a mobile baby shows more stranger anxiety because he is frightened by the new understanding that he can separate from his parent. A baby at this age also understands *object permanence*—he knows that his parent is somewhere, even if not in the room—and he cries when left with strangers as if to signal the alarm about the imposter.

Why Babies Do That

Why Do Some Babies Fear Dogs But Other Babies Love Them?

At eleven months old, every time my son would see a dog his whole body would shake with excitement and he would cry, "Oof oof!" Although he loved to look and point at them, he was always simultaneously terrified of dogs. If a dog came close to him for a friendly sniff, he would scream with terror.

It has been observed that babies who have regularly heard the sound of dogs barking in utero (and keep in mind a six-month-old fetus has already developed hearing) are unfazed by barking once they are born. When you have pets in your home—or in the neighborhood—and a baby watches you interact with them daily, he is less likely to fear them. The reverse is true too—if your baby has never heard the sound of a dog, he is more likely to startle at it and feel fear.

There are several other reasons why some babies fear dogs. From a baby's eye view, dogs are huge, rambunctious, slobbering, strange creatures who not only bark and growl but often monopolize adult attention. I was once walking with my three-month-old daughter and a Bernese mountain dog when some teenage girls stopped me on the street to admire the dog, not the baby. If a parent is wary of dogs and nervously scoops up a baby when a dog approaches, a baby may sense the parent's fear and feel apprehensive around them as well.

The old adage, "once bitten twice shy," applies to babies too. If a baby has had a bad experience with a dog, he will likely fear them. A baby's temperament also has a lot to do with it. My oldest daughter has always been spirited and courageous. One of her most memorable early experiences is when she was happily licked by a neighborhood dog. Oblivious to my apprehension (and unheeding of a growl), she would crawl or waddle up to any dog, large or small.

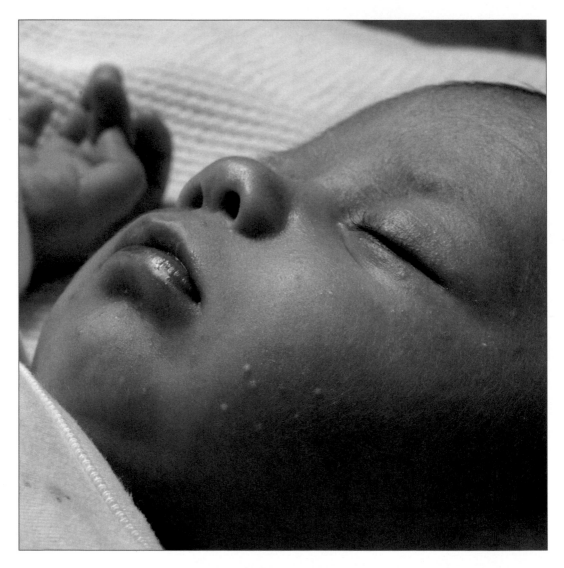

Why Babies Do That

Why Do Babies Get Acne?

Writer Anne Lamott nicknamed her newborn son "pizza face" when he broke out with a bad case of acne. Although we associate babies with soft clear skin, baby acne is actually very common. Some babies are born with it, and others develop a bad case of acne when they are a couple of weeks old. The pimples, which look like red raised bumps, usually appear heavily on both cheeks, as well as on the forehead, chin, and elsewhere. They sometimes have white or black heads to them, and the baby's skin will look very red, raw, and sore. As the pimples clear up and the skin dries out, the skin may be flaky and the pimples may scab.

The definitive answer to why babies get acne is still being debated but most experts agree that it has to do with exposure to a surge of fetal hormones passed through the placenta to the baby before birth and during labor. These hormones are also the reason that a newborn boy's scrotum looks enlarged and that a newborn girl's vulva is swollen, and may discharge a miniature "period." As strange as all of this is for a new parent, it is perfectly natural.

Baby acne can also be caused by skin irritations like baby drool or perfumed laundry detergents, and by exposure to medications from a nursing mother's breast milk (it has been hypothesized that chemicals found in anti-depressants, steroids, and birth control pills can cause acne). Too much exposure to the sun can cause prickly heat, a rash-like skin condition that looks like acne as well.

While newborn acne usually goes away in a couple of weeks, it may take months to clear up completely. Gently washing your baby's face with warm water and mild soap is the only treatment that doctors recommend.

Why Babies Do That

Why Do Babies Flail Their Little Arms and Legs Like Miniature Kickboxers?

The first time I saw a baby frantically flailing his arms and legs was as his mother carried him through the zoo in a front carrier. She was walking, and he was walking with her! At every age a baby needs exercise and this is one reason they flail their little arms and legs.

At six months, a baby who is waving his arms and kicking his legs has some control over his limbs. A baby at this age who is placed on his tummy may frantically pump his arms and legs to try to move forward or roll over. The exercise helps him tone his muscles and coordinate his movements.

Earlier, however, babies flail without being able to control their bodies, and a newborn will often scratch himself in the face or bonk you in the process. Newborns are very active and it seems like they are constantly flapping their little limbs, even in their sleep. This uncoordinated flailing is because a baby's motor system matures very slowly and it takes them a long time to coordinate even simple movements. Motor circuits in the brain are very complex and even a small movement involves a lot of complicated neural wiring. As a baby flails her arms and legs, these movements help her motor pathways develop. Flailing is also the result of a reflex they are born with, known as the *Moro* or *startle reflex*. If a newborn is startled suddenly, he will throw out his arms and legs, arch his back, and cry.

Older babies also flail their arms and legs to express emotion. They may be conveying their delight at seeing you or at spying the ever-elusive kitty, or they may be saying just the opposite. If the flailing is more like angry thrashing—stiff legs, whining, groaning—he is expressing his extreme frustration (kitty disappeared behind the couch again; he does not want to be strapped into the car seat).

Why Babies Do That

Why Do Babies Learn to Smile So Quickly and Like to Smile So Much?

Although many a proud parent has mistaken a newborn grimace or twitch for a full-fledged smile, babies do learn to smile at a remarkably young age. Some babies, especially those who are cooed to and smiled at often, will smile when they are only a few weeks old. The norm for social smiling, however, is about two months of age. Even babies who are blind will start smiling in response to a sound or a touch at this age, and studies of human babies across diverse cultural and social contexts have shown that the smile is universal.

In fact, very young babies will smile instinctively in response to a human face, no matter what expression is on that particular face at that time, which explains why my infant son would smile happily at his older sister even as she cried inconsolably. Between four and seven months, however, a baby becomes much more discerning with his smile, often reserving wide-mouthed drooly grins for familiar faces and flashing more tentative, suspicious smiles to unfamiliar people.

There's nothing more rewarding than the first time a baby smiles at you. That upturning of the corners of his mouth (which is often accompanied by a happy cooing sound and a little leg and arm flailing for emphasis) makes up for many a sleepless night and many a poopy diaper. When a baby smiles at you, your first instinct is to smile right back. By doing so, you are engaging a baby in one of his first conversations, showing delight at his expression, and reinforcing his smile. When a baby who smiles a lot is consistently smiled back it, he will often become a very smiley, happy baby.

The opposite is true too—though very young babies instinctively smile at human faces, a baby whose smile is not rewarded by smiles, nods, affection, and talk will soon lose interest in smiling. It is worth keeping in mind that though all babies smile—unless there is something developmentally wrong—some babies seem to be born serious. You may be the most playful person in the world but if baby has a somber temperament, it might not be easy to coax a smile from his lips, no matter how amusing your antics.

When babies smile they are telling you they are happy, inviting you to "talk" to them, suggesting a cuddle or some playtime. A baby will smile and flail in response to a familiar voice, indicating how much he loves you, how happy he is to see you, or how delighted he is that mealtime has finally arrived. No matter how urgently my son was wailing with hunger, when I settled him in place to nurse, he would flash me a gummy smile, sometimes accompanied by a little giggle, as a way of communicating his delight that it was finally time to eat. No wonder they have us wrapped around their little fingers!

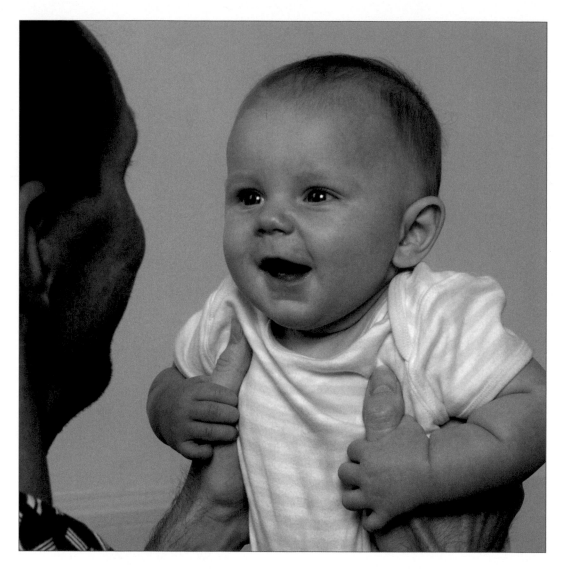

Why Babies Do That

Why Do Babies Look So Keenly at Human Faces?

As much as we love to look at babies, babies love to look at us. Even newborns with their feeble vision will look at a human face or at a picture in the shape of a human face (an oval with an arc for a mouth and two dots for eyes) for longer than they will look at anything else. Since these babies do not see faces in the womb, this behavior is thought to be innate.

There are many good reasons why a baby is born loving to look at human faces. Human faces are dynamic and responsive. When a baby looks at a face, the face moves and changes, the mouth opens and closes, the sound of a voice (which babies naturally love) emanates from it. Since adults often respond to a baby's keen look with a smile of love or approval, looking at a face provides a baby with a rewarding social experience and teaches her how to become a social creature, how to read emotions, and how to imitate another person (stick out your tongue, and baby may too).

By looking at a face a baby is setting the groundwork to learn language, emotional expression, emotional security, and responsiveness. The strong gaze that is shared by a baby and a mother is also a powerful bonding force. As mother and baby gaze into each other's eyes they get to know each other, learn to recognize each other, and feel love. By three months a baby will also follow the gaze of the person whose face she is looking at, which shows that she is learning to direct her attention to something another person finds interesting.

Forget mobiles. Forget the stuffed red puppy with hearts on its ears that plays an Elvis tune when you squeeze its belly. Forget flash cards. What a baby really wants to look at and play with is *you*.

Why Babies Do That

Why Do Babies Raise Their Eyebrows When They Look at You?

abies raise their eyebrows when they look at you because they're interested! As a baby looks at your face, he is trying to understand and imitate what he sees there.

Facial expressions, like raised eyebrows and drooly grins, are important nonverbal communication tools for a baby. Months or even years before a baby can master verbal communication, he gives adults a window into what he is thinking and feeling by his gestures and expressions, crying and coos. Since newborns across cultures universally exhibit contentment, distress, interest, and disgust, these emotions are thought to be innate, which brings us to eyebrow-raising.

When a baby raises his eyebrows, he is often expressing his curiosity or interest about something. Witness the seven-month-old in front of a toy box. Out comes a toy, up go the eyebrows. When he realizes he has seen the toy before, he hurls it away over his shoulder and digs for another toy. If the toy he pulls out the second time is unfamiliar to him, his eyebrows will stay raised for a few seconds longer as he examines his new find.

Indicative of interest, raised eyebrows also express a sister emotion: surprise. When an unexpected friend peers into the crib, or a knock on the door startles a baby, his eyes may widen and his eyebrows may raise in curious surprise.

Accompanied by a terrified look, raised eyebrows can also be indicative of fear (which is an emotion that researchers believe is learned through social interaction). When my son accidentally slipped under the water in the bathtub, he emerged with the most acute look of horror on his face. His eyebrows were raised, his eyes were bulging, and his face was a map of fear.

Why Babies Do That

Why Do Babies So Thoroughly Enjoy a Good Game of Peek-A-Boo?

There are many ways to play peek-a-boo. The classic version is to cover your face with your hands for a few seconds and then open your hands and cry "peek-a-boo!" The full body version involves hiding from a baby (by ducking under her crib or behind the door) and then popping out and yelling, "peek-a-boo!" Our favorite peek-a-boo game involves my husband clucking like a chicken and flapping his "wings" wildly on one side of the highchair. As he goes around to the back of the chair and out of sight he starts clucking much more quietly. Then he leaps out on the other side yelling "pauk pauk pauk!" (guaranteed to crack up any baby).

Babies love peek-a-boo for a variety of reasons. First, who wouldn't like seeing a grown-up act so smiley, energetic, and ridiculous? The peek-a-boo playing adult turns his whole attention to a baby, and all babies love receiving undivided attention. Babies are also naturally attracted to human faces, and peek-a-boo puts your face close to his. Babies also love smiles, which are a large part of the game, and babies love the sound of a grown-up's voice. That sing song "peek-a-boo" is fun for them to hear. Additionally, peek-a-boo is fun because of the element of surprise. A baby doesn't know exactly where or when a beloved face will peek through closed fingers. There is something positively thrilling to a baby about being surprised in this way.

Along with being fun, peek-a-boo also teaches babies the concept of *object permanence*. A baby learns that even if something is out of sight, it still exists.

Finally, a baby will quickly learn to play peek-a-boo back at you, covering his face with his hands or his head with a shirt. When he reveals himself and giggles he is making a joke—you thought I was gone but here I am! Ta dah!

Why Babies Do That

Why Do Babies Coo and Babble?

The reason a baby coos and babbles is because she is talking! We've all heard those sounds—the delightful mewling of a contented baby, the enthusiastic squeals of an excited baby, the *da-da-da-da* of an engaged baby. Even though babies can't talk to us in words, they do use lots of different sounds to communicate. Studies have shown that hearing-impaired babies will begin to babble at the same age as babies with normal hearing, suggesting that our brains are hard-wired to learn language even without auditory stimulation.

As amusing as the sound of a baby babbling is to an adult, it is even more so to the baby herself. At about four months of age, when many babies start babbling nonstop, babies will fascinate themselves by making new sounds with their own voices. Their babbling is their way of experimenting with language. It is also their way of having a conversation. If you ask a baby a question, she might respond with a nonsensical string of sounds and then pause, inviting you to respond in turn. At about the same age, babies will become more aware of the nuances of your voice, even if they can't understand the words you are saying. If you talk to them angrily, they may become silent or cry; if you speak in an excited happy voice, they may smile and babble back at you in the same tone.

Babies will also use babbling to get your attention. If you are reading the newspaper, talking on the phone, or playing with an older child, you might notice that the babbling increases. This is a baby's way of saying, "Look at me! Aren't I cute? Why not stop what you're doing and pay attention to me?"

Why Babies Do That

Why Do Babies Rub Their Eyes?

We've all seen a baby take his little fist and rub it vigorously into his eye, usually accompanied by a little yawn. Rubbing his eyes is a way that the baby has of telling us he is tired—that much is pretty obvious—but why eye rubbing?

As a baby gets tired his eyes get fatigued. When he rubs his eyes (as you would rub a sore arm muscle after playing baseball), he is relieving the soreness and tension in the muscles around the eyes, in the eyes, and in the lid. As a baby becomes tired his eyes also start to become dry. Having been exposed to air for a long time, the tear film that bathes the front of the eyes in a protective layer of tears begins to evaporate. Rubbing the eyes also stimulates tearing, which helps bring moisture back into the eyes.

Tiredness aside, there are some other possible reasons why babies rub their eyes. Babies love to touch every part of their bodies to learn how their bodies will respond. When you close your eyes and rub them, you know how you can see lights and patterns on the insides of your closed lids? When a baby who isn't tired rubs his eyes, it may be because of the fascinating visual stimulation he gets from doing so; he may be experimenting with what it's like to "see" with his eyes closed. Secondly, a baby may also rub his eyes if there is something irritating in them, like an eyelash. (If a baby is crying and continually rubbing his eyes, there might be something scratching his eye. Flush the eye with water and call the doctor.) Finally, maybe he's rubbing his eyes quite simply because they itch.

Why Babies Do That

Why Do Some Babies Bang Their Heads Against the Crib?

As disturbing as this behavior may seem to a concerned adult, the American Academy of Child Psychiatry has reported that up to 20 percent of otherwise normal children will bang their heads for some time. Head banging usually starts around six months of age, and it turns out that boy babies are three to four times more likely to bang their heads against the crib (or against the wall or the furniture) than girl babies, though no one really knows why.

The prevailing theory about why babies bang their heads against the crib is that it is a way to soothe themselves. Like thumb sucking, the rhythmic rocking that accompanies head-banging is lulling to the baby and helps him fall asleep or calm down after being upset. This theory posits that head-banging is a way for an anxious baby to relieve tension. Most babies, used to the rocking motion of their time in utero, enjoy swinging on swings and being rocked by their parents, and head-banging is akin to that kind of repetitive motion. Head-banging, like bouncing, swaying, and head-shaking, is also a way that babies can stimulate their vestibular system—the part of the brain responsible for our senses of balance and motion.

It has also been suggested that babies who bang their heads are not receiving enough soothing. Babies who are understimulated (because they are neglected, or because they are blind or deaf, for example) may bang their heads out of boredom or loneliness. In older babies, if head-banging is accompanied by other abnormal behaviors (or by the absence of several normal developmental behaviors), it may be a sign of autism.

Why Babies Do That

Why Do Babies Sleep During the Day and Wake Up at Night?

Being a baby, especially a newborn, is confusing. After living for nine months upside down floating in amniotic fluid in relative darkness, a newborn emerges into the noisy, bright, dry world outside the womb. When in utero a baby is constantly rocked by her mother's movement. Though some babies will be active while the mother is active (I remember riding my bicycle and having my daughter kicking in utero right along with me), usually the more active the mother, the more lulled the baby. So while you're up and about during the day, the baby sleeps. When you lie down at night, the lack of movement awakens and stimulates the baby. Then she does the cha-cha in your belly while you either slumber peacefully or, exhausted from insomnia, wonder why you ever got pregnant in the first place.

Since a baby in utero is used to sleeping during the day when the mother is active and kicking at night when the mother is quiet, as a newborn she will often continue this pattern for several weeks. It often seems that you could run a sledgehammer next to the bassinet during the day and she wouldn't wake up, but the minute you are ready for bed she's all open-eyed and fussy. Although some babies seem born to sleep at night, it commonly takes several months for a baby's circadian clock to adjust to the new world order.

A three or four-month-old baby's brain has matured enough to respond to environmental cues about night and day. But even a baby who is several months old will often have periods of alertness many times a night—waking up to nurse and to be reassured that someone is there with her. If it's driving you crazy, keep in mind that anthropologists believe this kind of wakefulness has been naturally selected. Human babies in times past were vulnerable to predators and other dangers, and sleeping lightly helped insure their survival.

There are some babies who seem to be born natural night owls, and simply like to be up at night. She may turn into the adult who falls asleep "for the night" as the alarm clock is signaling the start of a new day.

Additionally, everything from illness to the mastery of a new skill to a trip to see relatives can interfere with a baby's nighttime sleeping pattern and cause her to be up at night. No worries. In five or ten years, you'll all be getting more rest.

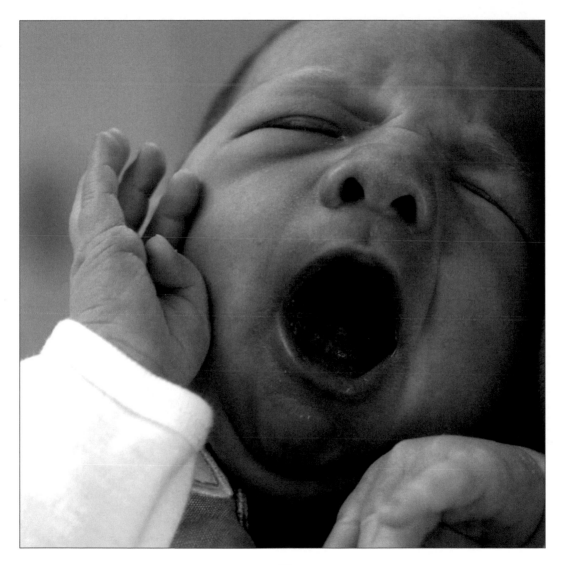

Why Babies Do That

Why Do Babies Resist Going to Sleep?

If you had just landed in a world where everything you saw, touched, smelled, and heard were new to you, would you want to go to sleep? No way. I'll let you in on a little secret: unlike your mother-in-law who suffers from insomnia, babies of all ages are of the firm opinion that sleep is overrated. Not only do they resist going to sleep, they resist staying asleep (unless you are holding them in just the right position—the one that makes your arm feel like it is about to fall off). And if they don't yet resist it, they will. My friend's newborn was a champion sleeper… until he woke up at six months of age and refused to sleep for the next two years.

Babies may also cry and protest at bedtime because they do not want to be separated from their parents and they feel scared or unprotected. Cross-cultural studies have shown that babies who live in cultures where they are carried most of the day and where they sleep next to their mothers at night seldom cry when it is time to go to sleep. Instead, they nurse to sleep or they become calm in response to the rhythmic breathing of an adult lying beside them. A human infant, like other primates, is genetically programmed to respond to adult care. If you lie down next to a baby at naptime or bedtime, you may notice a lot less resistance to going to sleep.

In the meantime, while you are walking around in a sleep-deprived haze, rest assured (tee hee) that your little resister is most likely getting the winks he needs.

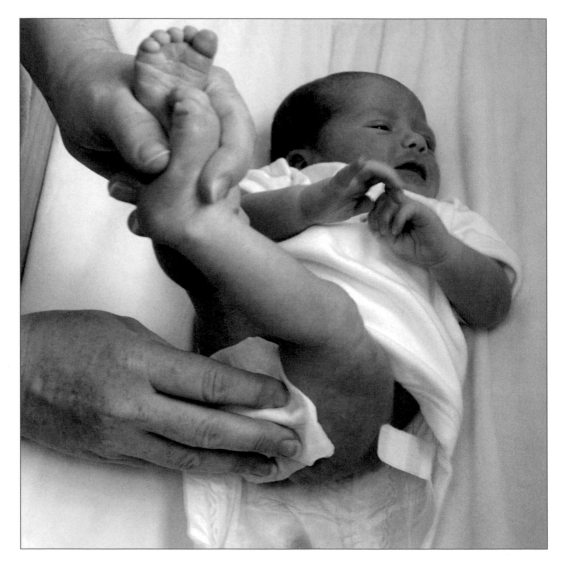

Why Babies Do That

Why Do Newborn Babies Have Poop That is Mustard-Colored and Seedy Looking?

Technically, they don't. Not at first anyway. At first a newborn passes *meconium*—a thick, tarry poop that is dark black or greenish-black and very smeary. Meconium is the substance that is in the baby's intestines at birth—a build up of mucus and debris from the fetus' time in utero—and it is passed during the first few days of life. A baby's poop will then undergo a change, becoming lighter and less smeary until it is a bright yellow color (like mustard or scrambled eggs) with little curds in it.

Breastfed baby poop is very loose and liquidy and sometimes smells sweetish, like breast milk itself or like apricots. It's very unusual looking to the untrained eye. This, combined with the fact that newborn babies can have explosive poops, or can poop many times an hour, often leads to full-fledged poop panic for many new parents. But the good news is that this watery yellow poop is remarkably easy to clean, and is actually not all that unpleasant (which is a good thing when you are changing six diapers an hour). The reason the poop looks this way is that breast milk is so nutritious to the baby and so easy to digest that most of it is absorbed by a baby's body. A formula-fed baby will have poop that is pastier and darker in color, and that gives off a stronger odor.

For as long as a baby is exclusively breastfed, the poop will have that mustardy look to it. When a baby starts eating solid foods, the consistency, texture, and color will change—and will vary dramatically depending upon what the baby is eating. It is very common for parents to worry about the frequency and the appearance of their baby's stools. But if a baby is acting happy and feeding normally, there is no need for alarm if she goes several days without pooping.

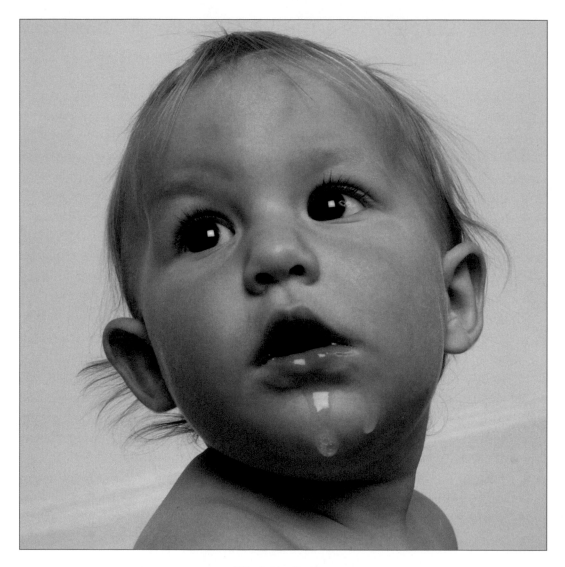

Why Babies Do That

Why Do Babies Drool?

I've heard babies referred to as veritable drool machines, a description that's not far from the truth. It seems like there is always something coming out of a baby's mouth—drool, spit up, half-chewed food. While this is a boon for companies that make baby bibs, it's a burden for the fastidious parent. (Moral of the story: don't be too fastidious.)

A baby usually starts to drool when tooth buds form under the gums and then erupt into teeth. Their gums may appear red and swollen and, if you run a finger along the gum line, you can usually feel the bumps of new teeth growing just under the surface. It is thought that teething patterns are hereditary. Babies usually get their first teeth between four and seven months of age, though this is just an average. It's not uncommon for a one-year-old to have a completely toothless, albeit charming, grin, and some newborn babies are born with one or two pearly whites already in their mouths. However, long before we see any teeth in a baby's mouth, the drooling is usually in full force.

Although drooling is most often linked to teething, a baby can drool at any time. Why? Whenever a foreign object is placed in the mouth, the mouth will begin producing saliva. The production of saliva is the first step in the digestive process and saliva works to break starches into their component sugars. When adults salivate, we swallow the excess saliva. When babies salivate, they do not sense the need to swallow, and the excess saliva dribbles down their chins instead. In their exuberance to taste and experience the world (one friend calls the baby's mouth his third hand), babies are often putting things in their mouths, jump-starting the drooling process.

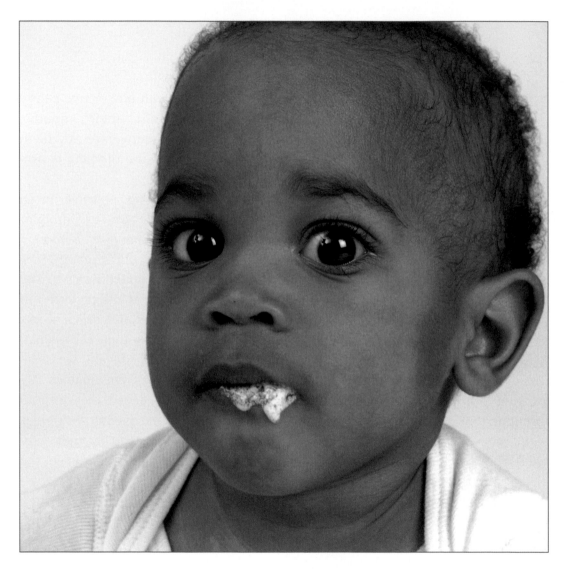

Why Babies Do That

Why Do Babies Spit Up So Often?

The first time you leave the house with a spit-up stain on your shirt, you will know you have just earned your official membership card to the I'm-The-Parent-Of-A-New-Baby Club. While many babies only spit up occasionally, others seem to be naturally more prone to doing it often (quick, where's the burp cloth?). Some champion spitter-uppers are so good at it that they manage to shoot the spit-up milk halfway across the room.

Babies spit up because babies spit up! It's part of their job. This notwithstanding, there are several reasons why. First of all, a baby's stomach is about the size of his fist. Think small. It can't hold a lot of milk and sometimes babies spit up because they have sucked down too much and their stomachs are over-full.

They may also spit up because they have swallowed a lot of air while they are suckling and as they burp the air out, they manage to upchuck most of their milk as well (or at least it seems that way). Spitting up may also be precipitated by jostling a full baby's tummy. *Wee!* goes the baby; up comes the nourishment.

The physiological reason for all this see-food is that the muscular valve between the esophagus and the stomach does not close tightly in young babies, as it does in adults. Instead, it is open enough that what is in the stomach often spills back out of the mouth, and dribbles down the chin. The baby doesn't mind though. And if he feeds often enough to get several double chins, you may even find spit-up cheese in the folds of his neck.

Why Babies Do That

Why Do Babies Like to Play With Their Own Poop?

I could hear from her happy coos that my nine-month-old was awake in her crib. Sometimes after a nap she would throw all of her stuffies onto the floor. Other times she would stand up and rattle the bars calling "dada, dada." But this day was different. Nothing could prepare me for what I would find in her room.

My daughter had opened up her diaper (a favorite baby pastime though one not explored in this book) and had found the contents of it to be fascinating. She had smeared poop all over the crib rails, the wall, and herself. She even had some around her mouth, which sent me straight to the phone to call poison control (she was fine). It turns out this behavior in human babies—like dogs who love to roll in the stuff—is not uncommon.

For babies who are very curious about everything in their world, poop is yet another object to explore. It is squishy like clay, it can color the furniture and the walls like finger paints, and it has a strong, interesting smell. Babies have no inhibitions. They have not yet learned the difference between "dirty" and "clean." To them poop, while it may be odoriferous, is not dirty. It's just interesting. Since babies put everything in their mouths, it makes sense that they would taste it too. As disgusting as it is to us, to a baby it's another learning experience.

The good news is that poop play is often a one-time thing. The bad news is that it may continue well into toddlerhood, when older babies become interested in all things potty related. Dismaying at best, this is all perfectly normal. However, if a three or four-year-old continues to play with his poop, it could be a sign of a more serious disturbance like autism.

Why Babies Do That

Why Are Babies So Fascinated by Balls?

An active five-month-old boy discovered a great game he could play with a kick ball. He crawled over to the ball, pushed it, and—surprise!—it rolled away. He scurried after it, and pushed it again. This game kept him occupied for a long time.

Balls are captivating to babies. As little scientists trying to understand the world around them, babies are always experimenting with toys. Most toys, like stuffed animals or blocks, have one or two dimensions, but balls are different. Unlike other toys, balls can do many things: they bounce, they roll, they sail through the air. Balls also come in many colors and sizes, and each with a different look, feel, smell, and textured surface. But no matter how differently they look or feel, all balls roll, a property that a baby will probably uncover on his own and find particularly curious. Babies can hold balls in their hands, gnaw on them, throw them, and make them move. When they pat the ball it may make a *boing boing* sound, just like when it bounces.

As a baby repeatedly tries to grasp a ball and it eludes him, he learns cause and effect, understanding for perhaps the first time how his actions change his environment. Additionally, playing with balls is often a social activity. Behold the adult whose smiling face remains as the ball rolls off, and it is no wonder that a baby will eagerly waddle after the ball just for the opportunity to bring it back to the grown-up to witness the smile again.

Why Babies Do That

Why Do Such Little Babies Like to Make Such a Big Mess?

How is it possible that such a small creature can be such a big juggernaut? At every age, babies seem to be naturally messy. A partial list of their mess-making activities includes: spitting up, drooling, hurling toys, ripping sheets of paper to shreds, throwing books onto the floor, dumping water out of cups, separating markers from their caps, scribbling on walls or on the favorite coffee table that is the only nice piece of furniture in the house (I've been there), hurling food out of the refrigerator, splashing water out of the tub, dribbling food, and smearing dirt on their foreheads.

Although it seems like they are making a mess to the adults who follow behind with mini-vacuums in hand, that's not actually what babies are doing. Babies are simply exploring their world, learning valuable lessons about object permanence, spatial relations, and the nature of things. The six-month-old who enjoys crinkling the mail, sucking on it, and tearing it is learning about the sound paper makes, the way it tastes, and the other properties it has; the ten-month-old who draws on the wall is discovering how markers work, as well as developing fine motor skills and practicing her grasp. As babies crawl or waddle around the house making a mess, their brains are actually taking in and processing lots of sensory information.

When a very small baby drops a toy, she probably won't notice it is gone. When the toy is out of sight to the baby, it no longer exists. As she grows, she starts to look for a dropped toy, understanding that the object exists even if she can't see it. This concept leads to a great mess-making game for babies, which is sometimes known as the "I-drop-it-you-pick-it-up game." Exasperating for the adult, perhaps, but a fascinating learning experience for the baby.

Why Babies Do That

Why Do Babies Plaster Pasta on Their Hair and Mash Bananas Into Their Cheeks?

When a baby first tastes food, be it rice mush or a mashed banana, he will probably respond with wide-eyed surprise. This first food is fascinating—its taste, smell, and texture are all new. Whether he puckers his lips, pumps his little tongue back and forth, or spits out the food entirely, the first time he tries some, a baby is sure to respond with almost scientific interest to the experience of eating. For a baby, there is so much to find out about food: what happens to peas when squashed between fingers? What does a banana do when mashed on cheeks? What happens when a sippy cup is dumped upside down? What kind of scribbles does yogurt make on the table?

One of the main reasons a baby makes such a mess with food is that he is exploring it. Unlike adults, a baby has no inhibitions (after all, why not plaster pasta in your hair?). For them, the food is not just for eating. It is also for smelling, touching, mashing, and scrutinizing.

To feed themselves babies must master a variety of skills. At first, your baby will hold a spoon very awkwardly, spilling most of its contents onto himself or the floor. Babies lack coordination and are not very goal oriented so they often miss their mouths and wind up with yogurt in their hair. If you look at the floor underneath the high chair, you may think that only a small portion of the food is actually going into (and staying in) his mouth.

Even very young babies come to understand that eating is a social experience. As you sit and eat with them, they may decide to feed you (half-chewed cucumber—yum!). Be assured that a baby's messy eating is universal. One day I ran into a friend, the mother of a seven-month-old, at the store. I decided not to tell her she had pureed carrots down the back of her shirt.

Why Babies Do That

Why Do Babies Cough and Splutter So Much When They are Eating?

We've already established that babies are very messy eaters and drinkers. While messy eating can be both cute and bothersome, there is something about that hacking baby cough at the table that strikes fear in a grown-up's heart. The baby will continue happily banging his sippy cup on the table while you rush to call 911. Though it seems terrifying, it's normal. As much as it worries us, all babies cough and splutter when they eat and drink.

Even newborns will cough and splutter as they nurse or have a bottle. This is partly because they have a lot of things to coordinate at the same time, including sucking and breathing. As they suck, their tongues are moving forward and backward while their jaws are moving up and down. It is difficult to suck milk out of a breast, and as they struggle to find a sucking pattern, their mouths may come off the nipple, making them inhale some droplets of milk, causing them to cough. A bottle-fed baby may cough if the milk is coming out too quickly, sending some of it down his windpipe.

As a baby grows, begins sitting up by himself, and starts eating solid foods, a whole new range of skills must be mobilized for effective eating and drinking. While a six- or seven-month-old baby may be eager to drink from a cup, he may not be coordinated enough to lift the cup, suck the water, swallow, and breathe without some of his drink going down his windpipe. Eating solids presents new challenges as well, and many babies will cough and gag on the texture of new foods, perplexed at the feel of them and unsure exactly how to chew and swallow.

The coughing itself is an effective way to dislodge anything that has inadvertently gone down the wrong tube. So come back to the table. As long as he is coughing, your baby is not choking.

Why Babies Do That

Why Do Babies Love to Be Bounced and Jiggled?

It's not just babies who love to be bounced and jiggled, older children and grown-ups love it too (think swings, rollercoasters, bumper cars, bungee jumping, and vibrating water beds). A love of repetitive movement is present in even very small babies because of something called the *vestibular system*, the part of the brain that senses motion and balance. As a baby grows, her vestibular system matures, helping her to keep her head upright or to stay standing without holding on to a parent's leg.

When a newborn is crying inconsolably, repetitive movement like bouncing or jiggling is sometimes the only thing that will comfort her. This bouncing seems to distract her from her sadness and help her become quiet and alert. It also makes her sleepy. If she is fussing because she is resisting sleep, bouncing can be the best way to soothe her.

Some researchers believe that one of the reasons babies love to be bounced is that the movement itself helps improve a baby's sense of balance and her ability to perceive movement. By stimulating the vestibular system, bouncing may actually help a baby improve gross motor skills like crawling and walking.

My uncle used to throw his baby boy up in the air and catch him, causing my cousin to squeal with delight. Babies love attention, smiles, movement, and human contact. Being bounced by a grown-up often provides all four at the same time. When a baby bounces by herself she can also learn cause and effect. A baby in a jumper, for example, learns that when she bends her legs and pushes off she can make herself soar upwards.

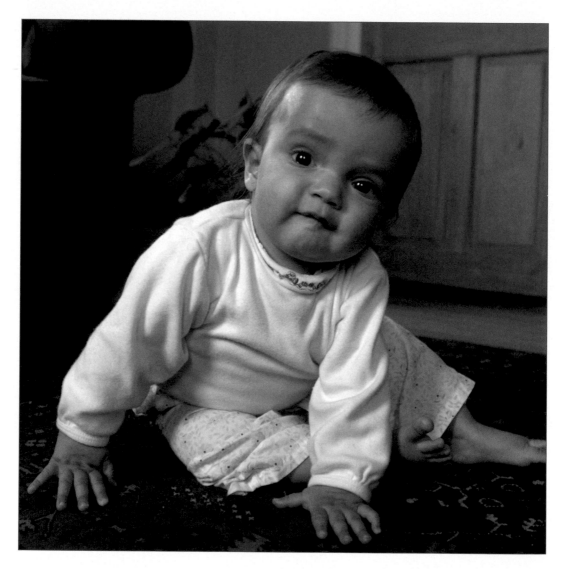

Why Babies Do That

Why Do Babies Tripod Before
They Sit Up Straight?

A newborn is a floppy creature whose muscles are flaccid. As a baby grows, he strengthens muscle tone, masters control of his limbs, and learns how to make his body move the way he wants it to. Something as seemingly straightforward as sitting involves a range of muscles and muscle control, as well as balance, and a baby actually starts working toward sitting up several months before he is able to. In order to sit up unaided, the baby has to have strong back and neck muscles and a sense of balance in his torso, head, and neck.

If you hold an infant's hands while he is lying down and help him into a sitting position, you can see his eyes go wide with wonder at the new view. The first step toward this fascinating new way of seeing the world is strong neck muscles and a balanced head. Once the baby learns to hold his head up, he will start working on strengthening his upper body by arching his back and lifting his chest when lying on his stomach. Once the baby is strong enough to lift up his chest, sitting upright is close at hand. But though he may have the strength, he may not have the balance. Tripoding—or sitting on his tush with his arms straight out in front of him and his hands on the floor—is a way for a baby to sit up by himself before he has the balance to stay sitting unaided. Expect a tripoding baby to tumble often to one side or another (some propping with pillows will help keep him stable.)

When a baby can finally sit by himself, he'll have much to do—he can stare at his hands as they move in front of him, play with toys, chew on teething rings, watch you putter more easily, and examine the world from his happy seat on the floor. Try to enjoy it while it lasts as crawling will be just around the corner.

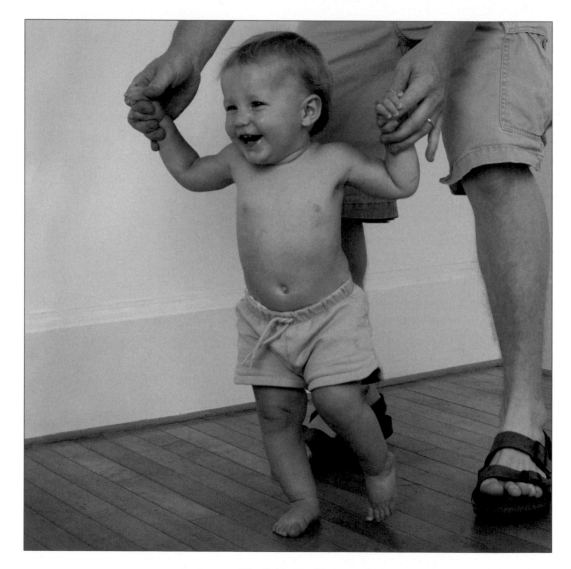

Why Babies Do That

Why Do Babies Waddle When They Walk?

When he first learned to walk, my son would clunk one unsteady foot down after the other, waddling forward and waving a hand in the air to the sound of music only he could hear. He walked so uncertainly that he looked like a conductor directing an orchestra on a listing ship. Although he was walking by one year, my oldest daughter did not take a single step by herself until she was 15 months old.

Some babies begin walking as early as eight or nine months of age. Others cannot stand up by themselves until they are a year old. If your baby was born to move, she might bend all her energy toward learning how to walk. But if she is the kind of person who prefers books and babbling to frantic mobility, she may not be walking much before her second birthday. For months before they begin walking, babies are pulling up on furniture, standing on your lap and bouncing up and down, and generally working to strengthen and coordinate the muscles involved in moving themselves forward on their own two legs.

As hard as they are trying to learn to walk, those first baby steps are shaky indeed. They may lift their knees up higher than they need to, and thud the front part of each foot down in a toe-heel combination at first. In addition, when they start walking, babies keep their feet quite far apart in order to improve their balance. This stance, combined with unsteady limbs (many babies who know how to walk seem not to understand how to bend their own legs), and a big old diaper on their tushies, make a baby's walk look like a duckling's waddle. As babies gain more control of their limbs and find a steadier balance, the signature waddle disappears (along with their pudgy thighs, the diapers, and the drooly smiles). And no matter how slowly every day goes by now, you'll miss it all.

Why Babies Do That

Why Do Babies Love to Boogie?

Making music and dancing are two activities that set human beings apart from other animals. Indeed, across cultures adults and children alike enjoy music together. There is nothing like the delight a small baby feels when you take him in your arms and dance with him. As a baby gets older, he will want to dance by himself: wiggling his booty, kicking his legs, waving his arms, jumping and hopping around, and generally boogying down to the music.

One look at a dancing baby is enough to confirm the very simple explanation of why babies love to boogie: Dancing is fun! Dance music is usually lively and exciting. A baby's heart rate goes up when he dances, his breathing quickens, and the movement to the music makes him feel joyous. Just like with adults, the exercise a baby gets from dancing produces endorphins in his body—chemicals that make him feel good.

Dancing is also a social activity. Either adults will be on the sideline cheering (and, as we've mentioned, babies love to be the center of attention) and providing positive reinforcement for the future Fred Astaire, or they will be dancing right alongside him. While he boogies, he revels in the new ways that he can coordinate his movements, laughs when he plops to the ground unexpectedly, and finds the unexpected quirky steps of the siblings or grown-ups dancing with him to be uproariously funny.

Why Babies Do That

Why Do Babies Always Try to Put Their Fingers in Electric Sockets?

Once babies are crawling and walking they seem to gravitate toward danger. Unsteady rocks? Let me see if I can climb up them. Burning hot stove? Hmm, what will happen if I lie my cheek against it? Poisonous chemical? If I could just get this top off I'd drink some. While babies seem to constantly find the only cabinet in the house that isn't locked, there does seem to be something especially interesting about wall sockets. Whether trying to put their fingers or the tines of a fork in them, many babies are particularly fond of the dangerous allure of the electric socket.

For one thing, the electric socket is at just the right height for a crawling baby, as if it were placed there just for her. She can see its inviting holes and curious-looking texture without straining. Second, she sees grown-ups putting things into and out of the plugs. Babies learn much of their behavior by imitating adults, so why not do what a grown-up does and put something sharp into the socket?

Additionally, when a baby does put her fingers in the socket, grown-ups take notice. She soon understands that this particular play place is an attention getter, and she may go back to it time and again for that reason alone.

Why Babies Do That

Why Do Many Babies Say "Da Da" Before They Say "Ma Ma"?

The first sounds that babies learn to say tend to be consonants made with the lips: p, b, and m. The next consonants they learn are those formed with the gums and teeth: t, d, and n. Many babies will chain consonants and vowels together and make sounds like "ga-ga-ga" and "da-da-da" from very early on, experimenting with sounds and with the interesting ways they are moving their mouths. In the midst of all this nonsensical noise making, many babies say "da-da" over "ma-ma," and will repeat the word "da-da" consistently long before they ever say "ma-ma."

Before you fathers burst with too much pride, however, you should be aware that even though your baby is repeating what sounds like a distinct word to you, the baby might just have come up with a generic "dada" for everything. If baby calls you "dada" and also calls her spoon "dada" and further refers to the cat as "dada," your baby is not saying "daddy" but rather saying "thing" and using the word "dada" as a generic catch-all.

Once a baby actually says "dada" to mean "daddy," she may so delight in the association of the word with her father that she will call every man who walks down the street "dada," another disconcerting trend for parents but one that makes good sense to the baby. In this case, "dada" means "man," or even "person," and perhaps "father."

My oldest daughter, a prodigious talker, called me "dada" for more than six months and no amount of praising, correcting, or cajoling could teach her differently. When she finally learned to say "mama," she was so happy with the switch that she started calling my husband Mama as well.

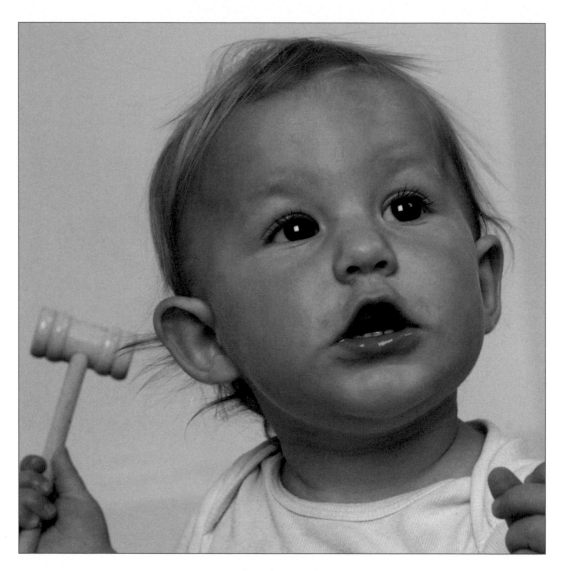

Why Babies Do That

Why Do Babies Learn Languages So Easily?

The ability to learn language is hard-wired into our brains, and recent research has shown that newborns will actually prefer the cadence of their native language at birth, suggesting that some language learning has started in utero. From a very early age, babies are better able to hear the sounds of foreign languages than adults are. After birth, they are very responsive to every language—a human voice is always a good way to get a baby's attention. Their preference for speech over other kinds of sounds, as well as their ability to distinguish different sounds, is thought to be innate. Since babies are able to hear foreign sounds so well, early life is the best time to learn a first language, and a second and a third.

As children grow, they get better at their native language and it becomes harder and harder for them to discriminate foreign sounds. This concept is called *cognitive crowding*, and, although no one really knows why, it is thought that once a native language is firmly entrenched in the brain, that knowledge crowds out the ability to hear the sounds of other languages as well.

Babies and young children, however, do not have this problem. Until age six, children are very receptive to language learning. Then the brain gradually starts closing up. After the end of puberty, around age 16, it becomes harder (though, of course, not impossible) to learn a foreign language and foreign pronunciation well. What does all this mean? If you still have a young baby at home, it's time to buy your plane tickets. Destination: Paris.

Why Babies Do That

Why Do Some Babies Say Their First Word in the First Year While Other Babies Don't Start Talking Until They Are Two or Three?

We've all heard that Einstein did not speak until he was three years old, and many of us know little nine-month-old babies who are already saying several words. Why such a discrepancy?

The obvious reason is that every baby learns to speak at her own pace. However, there is ample evidence that girl babies, on average, talk about one month earlier than boy babies. Interestingly, this difference will continue beyond babyhood with girls scoring consistently higher than boys on verbal fluency tests throughout life.

Still, there is a tremendous amount of individual variation in the rate that babies learn to speak, and this variation is thought to be both hereditary and environmental. Most adults, especially mothers, seem instinctively to talk to babies in a way that babies can understand. They use nouns instead of pronouns ("Mommy's going to get the baby dressed now," for example); they repeat words and phrases; and they talk more slowly. By engaging a baby in verbal exchanges even before the baby can speak intelligibly, the adult is helping the baby learn to speak. In general, the more you ask your baby questions, point out newly fallen leaves and brightly colored birds, allow her time to respond, and repeat your baby's noises back to her, the quicker she'll be talking. Although all children will learn to speak, babies who are in an environment where adults seldom talk to them may have delayed speech.

One of my daughters was speaking in almost full sentences by the time she was 18 months old. At the same age, my son could only say a handful of words. Environment or heredity? It's hard to make a convincing case for either. Moral of the story: don't compare your children.

Why Babies Do That

Why Do Babies Love to be Cuddled?

It's not just babies who like cuddling, it's grown-ups too! There's nothing quite like sitting in a rocking chair holding a baby, enjoying her soft skin and sweet smell. Cuddling is essential for bonding and for insuring that a baby thrives. So why does everybody love a hug-fest?

When a baby is held close, she feels protected, safe, and loved. When you cuddle her, she can feel and hear your heart beat—a sound that is both familiar and comforting. As smell is one of the most developed senses in very small babies, she also benefits from being able to smell you as you cuddle. As babies get older and become more mobile, they may often come back for a quick cuddle—as a way to reassure themselves that they haven't gone too far away.

The importance of cuddling shouldn't be underestimated. Although psychologists once believed that babies sought out their mothers only because they provided them with nutrition, a series of experiments on rhesus monkeys in the 1960s showed that primates need comfort more than they need food. Baby monkeys were put in a cage with two different wire "mothers": one was made of wood and wire only and provided milk, and one was covered with terry cloth but provided no milk. Contrary to expectation, the terrified baby monkeys spent most of their time clinging to the cloth "mother," suggesting that the nurturing aspect of mothering is more important to development than providing sustenance.

Cuddling, it turns out, actually stimulates growth hormones and reduces stress hormones. Physical contact enhances the immune system, helps babies grow healthy and strong, and gives them a sense of emotional well-being. Many studies have shown that babies who are cuddled are better adapted socially and intellectually than their counterparts who are deprived of affection. So put this book down right now and go hug a baby!

Why Babies Do That

Why Do Babies Always Look So Darn Cute?

When you are on a crowded airplane and your baby is howling, the other passengers might not agree that babies always look so cute. But despite your grumpy uncle's insistence that he does *not* like babies, baby humans (and other baby animals) look pretty darn cute to most adults.

There are many reasons we think babies are cute. Research has shown that adult humans are programmed to find a baby's big-head-to-small-body ratio and their big eyes attractive. The big-head-to-small-body ratio is also the reason we exclaim over baby sheep at the farm and baby monkeys at the zoo. And what kitten or puppy's big eyes haven't melted even the gruffest animal hater's heart? For humans, this innate programming insures the survival of our species, giving us a reason to protect these otherwise very vulnerable and helpless creatures.

Babies are adorable for all sorts of other reasons too. They smell good. They have round chubby cheeks just waiting to be pinched, and ridiculously distended bellies just asking to be tickled. They are so helpless and little that they just beg to be cared for. Their skin is soft and supple—a real pleasure to feel. And they love us! They are fascinated by our faces and spend a lot of time looking and smiling at us.

Another reason we like our own babies (or babies related to us) is that they often resemble us or the people we love most in the world. Gazing into a baby's curious eyes brings us back to a time when we were little. Being with a baby is a chance to recreate our own childhoods or offers a chance to do over what might not have been done so well in the first place.

When a little baby holds out his arms for the first time and calls out to us, it's impossible not to feel a rush of love and a surge of joy in the face of such cuteness.

Why Babies Do That